Favourite FAST *Recipes*

Anne O'Donovan
in association with
Penguin Books

A PENGUIN POCKET SERIES BOOK

First published in 1992 by
Anne O'Donovan Pty Ltd
Level 3, 171 La Trobe Street Melbourne 3000

Reprinted 1992 (twice)
Reprinted 1994, 1995

Written with Angie Burns Gaté
Edited by Margaret Barrett
Designed by Lynn Twelftree
Illustrated by Lynn Twelftree
Set in Palatino by Post Typesetters, Queensland
Printed by McPherson's Printing Group
Distributed by Penguin Books Australia Ltd

National Library of Australia
Cataloguing-in-publication entry

Gaté, Gabriel, 1955–
    Gabriel Gaté's favourite fast recipes.

    Includes index.
    ISBN 0 14 016987 3.

    1. Cookery (Natural foods). 2. Quick and easy cookery.
    I. Title. II. Title: Favourite fast recipes. (Series: Penguin
    pocket series).

641.563

CONTENTS

INTRODUCTION

Gabriel, what is your favourite dish? During my busy weekly activities this has to be the question I am most often asked. It is not easy to answer, as I have so many favourites. Some are family favourites and some are for special occasions with friends. Then there are the summer and winter favourites . . . So it is really a matter of mood, occasion and season. Some of my everyday favourites have the distinction of being quick to prepare, and this is the reason why I have put the fast recipes I like best into this little book. Its small size gives it the advantage of being easy to carry around in pocket, handbag or glovebox so that you can refer to it at any time, perhaps while shopping or during your lunch break, and make a snap decision on what to cook for your next meal.

Importantly for me, the recipes follow the dietary recommendations of leading Australian health organisations such as the Anti-Cancer Council and the Heart Foundation. We are advised to eat a wide variety of foods, to use a minimum of fat, salt and sugar in our cooking, to keep our weight down, and to eat plenty of high-fibre foods such as vegetables, wholegrain cereals and fruit. I have selected recipes that are simple to prepare, and most of whose ingredients are readily available from your local supermarket, butcher, fish-monger and greengrocer.

The majority of dishes, once you are familiar with the recipe, will demand less than thirty minutes of your time from beginning to end. A handful take a little longer to cook but the preparation is easy. You will find recipes for salads, vegetables, soups, pasta, fish, chicken and meat, all with a special touch that makes them popular. Lastly there are the desserts, which I know will delight many of you. In between the recipes I have included some handy hints to save shopping time and make you more efficient in the kitchen. As you become a better cook you will enjoy cooking more and more.

I hope that Gabriel Gaté's Favourite Fast Recipes will become your favourites too.

Bon appétit!

Gabriel Gaté

ACKNOWLEDGEMENTS

I am happy to say that *Favourite Fast Recipes*, like my other books *Family Food, Smart Food* and *Good Food Fast*, has been a team effort, and I wish to thank all who contributed in one way or another. My biggest thanks go to my wife, Angie Burns Gaté, for her enormous support. I must also thank Angie's mother, Clare Burns, and our sons, Sebastian and Michael, for their help. A special *merci* goes to my cookery assistants, Jane McEvoy and Philip Neil, and I want to express my appreciation to my publisher, Anne O'Donovan; my editor, Margaret Barrett; and to Amanda Stephens.

A number of the recipes that first appeared in *Family Food, Smart Food* and *Good Food Fast* have been adapted for inclusion here. Those books were published in association with the Anti-Cancer Council of Victoria, for whose continuing support and cooperation I am very grateful.

Family favourites

The majority of the recipes in this section are for main-course dishes based on chicken, fish, and various meats or cuts of meat that do not take long to prepare. Many of the recipes include both meat and vegetables, and you need only cook potatoes, pasta, rice or some other accompaniment of your choice to create a truly balanced meal.

VEGETABLES GALORE

Cheese ravioli and red pepper salad

For a lovely effect, use green spinach-flavoured cheese ravioli and red capsicum. If fresh ravioli is unavailable you can substitute frozen varieties. This salad is simple to prepare yet substantial enough to serve as a light main course.

SERVES ABOUT 4

1 red capsicum
2 tomatoes
2 tsp balsamic vinegar
1 tbsp olive oil
1 clove garlic, chopped
freshly ground black pepper
250 g (9 oz) fresh green ravioli
6 basil leaves, finely sliced

METHOD

Halve, seed and wash capsicum and slice very finely.

Wash tomatoes and cut into small pieces.

In a salad bowl mix capsicum and tomato with vinegar, oil, garlic and a little pepper.

Bring a large saucepan of lightly salted water to the boil and cook ravioli until tender (it takes 8 to 12 minutes, depending on the dryness of the pasta) or cook according to packet instructions.

Drain cooked ravioli and cool in very cold water. Drain again and gently shake to remove as much water as possible. Then gently stir ravioli into salad bowl with finely sliced basil, and serve.

Herbed chicken salad

You can be very creative with this dish by using other leftover meat or fish and a different mixture of herbs or vegetables.

SERVES 4

2 small carrots
¼ lettuce
1 capsicum
2 tomatoes
about 400 g (14 oz) leftover roast chicken
1 tsp mustard
a pinch of salt
freshly ground black pepper
1 tsp red wine vinegar
1 tbsp olive oil
1 tbsp chopped chives
½ tbsp chopped tarragon
1 tbsp chopped parsley
about 15 coriander leaves

METHOD

Wash, peel and microwave or steam carrots, then dice them. Wash and shred lettuce. Halve, seed and wash capsicum and cut it finely. Wash and dice tomatoes.

Trim chicken of skin and fat and slice thinly.

In a small bowl mix mustard, salt, a little pepper, vinegar and oil.

In a large bowl toss chicken, carrots, chives, tarragon and parsley with half the dressing, and spoon into the centre of a serving platter.

Using the same bowl, toss lettuce, capsicum and tomatoes with remaining dressing and spoon this around chicken. Sprinkle washed coriander leaves over chicken and serve.

COOKING TIP

A salad spinner is effective in drying lettuce and other leaves before they are tossed in a dressing.

Basmati rice, fennel and tuna salad

You will enjoy the aromatic combination of basmati rice, fennel and tuna – it's a refreshing favourite.

SERVES 4

1½ cups basmati rice
2 pinches of salt
½ tsp olive oil
1 globe of fennel
1 apple, preferably Granny Smith
1 red capsicum
½ white onion
1 can tuna in oil (about 200 g)
freshly ground black pepper
1 tsp vinegar
2 tbsp chopped parsley
12 cashew nuts

METHOD

Place rice in a saucepan with 2¼ cups of cold water, a pinch of the salt and olive oil. Bring to boil, cover and simmer for 17 minutes. The rice is cooked by the absorption method. Allow rice to cool when it is cooked.

Wash and dice fennel, apple and capsicum. Chop onion.

Strain tuna to separate the fish from the oil. Reserve tuna oil. In a small bowl, mix remainder of salt and a little pepper with vinegar and tuna oil. Stir in parsley and onion.

Place rice, fennel, apple and capsicum in a salad bowl and toss with dressing. Sprinkle with tuna and cashew nuts and serve.

Cucumber and celery salad with a mint and yoghurt dressing

This salad is very refreshing. In summer it is lovely with grilled fish or meat, and it is a popular accompaniment to satay.

SERVES 4

4 sticks celery
1 small European cucumber
1 carrot
juice of ½ lemon
a pinch of salt
freshly ground black pepper
2 tbsp yoghurt
1 clove garlic, chopped
8 mint leaves, finely sliced
2 tbsp walnuts, chopped

METHOD

Wash celery and slice thinly. Peel and halve cucumber, remove seeds, and finely slice it. Peel and grate carrot.

In a salad bowl mix lemon juice, salt and a little pepper with yoghurt, garlic and mint. Toss all vegetables in dressing and sprinkle with chopped walnuts just before serving.

Dressing with an Asian touch

We are all familiar with French and Italian dressings, but Asian versions less so. Here is a simple one. In a bowl mix a little freshly ground black pepper with the juice of half a lemon, ½ tsp sesame oil, 2 tsp soy sauce, 2 tsp peanut oil and half a clove of chopped garlic. And voilà! – an Asian dressing to serve with shredded cabbage or any other vegetable, with fish or with meat.

Lentil salad with cherry tomatoes and chives

This satisfying salad is a light vegetarian meal in itself, especially when served with bread. I have enjoyed it many times in a toasted multigrain sandwich.

SERVES 4

a 400 g (14 oz) can cooked lentils
about 250 g (9 oz) cherry tomatoes
a pinch of curry powder
a pinch of salt
freshly ground black pepper
1 tsp red wine vinegar
1 tbsp olive oil
½ white onion, chopped
1 Granny Smith apple
1 stick celery
2 tbsp chopped chives

METHOD

Drain lentils.

Wash and halve cherry tomatoes or leave whole if you prefer.

In a small bowl mix curry powder, salt and a little pepper with vinegar, then mix in oil and onion.

Peel and dice apple. Wash and finely slice celery.

Place lentils, cherry tomatoes, apple and celery in a salad bowl and very gently toss with dressing and chives.

COOKING TIP

Canned beans and lentils are a great standby if you don't have time to soak any pulses; look for the low-salt varieties.

Stir-fried vegetables with pork mince and rice noodles

Rice noodles are popular with most people. The Chinese call them 'rice stick' and add them to many stir-fry dishes.

SERVES 4

150 g (5½ oz) rice noodles
½ cauliflower
1 red capsicum
½ white onion
1½ tbsp sunflower or other polyunsaturated oil
300 g (11 oz) lean pork mince
1 tbsp soy sauce
½ tsp chilli sauce (optional)
4 spring onions cut into small pieces

METHOD

Cook rice noodles in boiling water, following instructions on pack (it takes about 4 minutes).

Cut cauliflower into bite-size pieces.

Halve, seed and wash capsicum and cut into bite-size squares. Dice onion.

Heat 1 tbsp of the oil in a hot wok and on high heat stir-fry cauliflower, capsicum and onion for 2 minutes. Add 3 tbsp water, stir, and cover wok with either a lid or foil; cook for about 2 minutes or until cauliflower is just done. Transfer vegetables to a plate.

Add remaining oil to wok and on high heat stir-fry pork for about 2 minutes. Stir in soy sauce, vegetables and noodles and reheat. Season with chilli sauce and sprinkle with spring onion before serving.

Tandoori-style vegetables

This dish of roast vegetables coated with a spicy yoghurt paste is very flavoursome. The vegetables take about 40 minutes to cook but preparation is quite fast.

SERVES 4

1 tbsp low-fat yoghurt
1 tsp grated ginger
¼ tsp freshly ground black pepper
¼ tsp chilli powder
2 tsp paprika
1 tsp curry powder
1 tsp polyunsaturated oil
1 tsp lemon juice
about 250 g (9 oz) pumpkin
2 small sweet potatoes
2 medium carrots

METHOD

Preheat oven to 200°C/400°F.

In a bowl mix yoghurt, ginger, pepper, chilli, paprika, curry powder, oil and lemon juice.

Peel and wash pumpkin, sweet potatoes and carrots. Cut pumpkin into four pieces and halve sweet potatoes and carrots.

Coat vegetables with yoghurt preparation. Place them on an oiled oven rack resting in an oven dish and roast until tender (about 40 minutes). Turn vegetables a couple of times during cooking.

COOKING TIP

Really fresh young vegetables have the sweetest flavour and cook in no time.

SOUPS

Zuppa italiana

This Italian-style soup is a light meal that we enjoy for lunch in winter served with crusty bread. The addition of cooked chicken or cooked dried beans makes it heartier.

SERVES 4

2 small carrots
100 g (3½ oz) French beans
1 zucchini
1 small stick celery
1 cup broccoli (or cauliflower) pieces
a little olive oil
½ tsp finely chopped rosemary
5 cups water
1 cup vermicelli or other small pasta
6 basil leaves
1 clove garlic
1 tbsp grated parmesan cheese
freshly ground black pepper

METHOD

Trim and peel carrot.

Top and tail beans.

Trim zucchini.

Wash celery and broccoli (or cauliflower).

Cut carrot, zucchini and celery into slices and cut beans and broccoli into bite-size pieces.

Brush a saucepan with oil and gently fry rosemary, carrot, zucchini and celery for a few minutes. Add beans, broccoli and water and boil for 2 minutes before adding pasta. Stir well, return to boil and cook for 10 minutes.

Finely chop basil and garlic. Stir basil, garlic and parmesan into soup and season with a little pepper just before serving.

Winter leek soup with rice

Served with bread, this hearty soup becomes a light meal.

SERVES 6

2 leeks
1 small carrot
200 g (7 oz) mushrooms
a little polyunsaturated oil
½ cup brown rice
6 cups chicken stock or water
a pinch of salt
2 tbsp chopped parsley
freshly ground black pepper

COOKING TIP

Keep chicken stock in
the freezer as the basis
for a quick, flavour-
some soup: the perfect
one-dish meal.

METHOD

Remove damaged or stringy outer leaves of leeks and trim off most of the tougher green part, shortening the roots at the base. Then cut leeks in four lengthwise, leaving base intact, and wash thoroughly in lukewarm water to flush out dirt. Slice thinly.

Peel carrot and cut into small dice; wash and dice mushrooms.

Brush a saucepan with a little oil and gently fry leeks, carrot and mushrooms for a few minutes. Add rice, chicken stock or water and salt, and cook for 45 minutes or until rice is done.

Blend half the soup to a purée and return it to saucepan. Bring to boil and, before serving, stir in chopped parsley and season with pepper.

Old-fashioned split pea and ham soup

This dish was popular for dinner in Europe in the old days when meat was scarce. It was of course served with lots of bread.

SERVES 4–6

½ brown onion
2 carrots
about 1 cup pumpkin flesh
a little olive oil
12 cummin seeds
a few sprigs parsley, a sprig thyme and ½
    bay leaf, washed and tied together with
    kitchen string
4 cups cold water
a 400 g (14 oz) can split peas
100 g (3½ oz) ham
freshly ground black pepper
about 2 tbsp chopped parsley

METHOD

Peel and dice onion, carrots and pumpkin.

Brush a saucepan with a little oil and fry onion, carrots, pumpkin and cummin seeds for a few minutes. Add herbs and cold water. Bring to boil and cook for about 15 minutes. Add split peas and cook for a further 15 minutes.

Trim ham and cut it into small strips.

Blend half the soup to a purée then return it to the pot. Bring to boil, season with pepper and, just before serving, add ham and parsley.

COOKING TIP

If you make a double quantity of soup you can freeze half to reheat for an instant meal later.

Chunky turkey soup

*This soup is a one-pot meal and therefore easy to prepare.
Use any vegetables you have on hand if you lack those
suggested. Turkey is now available all year round from
markets and poultry specialists, but you can replace it
with chicken or duck if you wish.*

SERVES ABOUT 4

1 small leek
2 medium carrots
1 zucchini
1 stick celery
100 g (3½ oz) cauliflower
a little olive oil
6 cups water
1 cup pasta (e.g. butterfly, springs)
300 g (11 oz) deboned
   turkey pieces (fillet or thigh)
1 tbsp chopped parsley
freshly ground black pepper

METHOD

Cut leek in four lengthwise, leaving root intact. Wash leek thoroughly in lukewarm water to remove grit, then slice it.

Peel carrots and slice thinly.

Wash zucchini and celery and slice thinly.

Wash cauliflower and separate florets into bite-size pieces.

Brush a saucepan with a little oil and on medium heat gently fry leek, carrot, zucchini and celery for 2 minutes. Add water and return to boil. Add pasta, stir well, bring to boil and cook for about 5 minutes.

Meanwhile skin turkey and cut into bite-size pieces.

Add cauliflower to soup and boil for 3 minutes. Add turkey pieces and stir well. Keep soup hot for 5 minutes to allow turkey pieces to cook, but avoid boiling as this will make them tough.

Season soup with parsley and a little pepper before serving.

Creamed leek and mushroom soup

To make the texture of this soup rich and creamy I have cooked it with rice. If you eat it with bread it will add up to a light meal, not just part of one.

SERVES 6

2 leeks
1 small carrot
200 g (7 oz) mushrooms
a little polyunsaturated oil
½ cup short-grain white rice
6 cups chicken stock or water
a pinch of salt
2 tbsp chopped parsley or chives
freshly ground black pepper

COOKING TIP

Fresh mushrooms do
not need peeling:
simply wipe them with
a cloth or wash them
briefly in water.

METHOD

Remove damaged or stringy outer leaves of leeks and trim off most of the tougher green part. Shorten the roots at the base, then cut leeks in four lengthwise, leaving base intact, and wash thoroughly in lukewarm water to flush out dirt. Slice thinly.

Peel carrot and cut it into small dice; wash and finely slice mushrooms.

Brush a saucepan with the oil and gently fry leeks, carrot and mushrooms for a few minutes. Add rice, chicken stock or water and salt, and cook for 45 minutes or until rice is done.

Blend two-thirds of the soup to a purée and return it to saucepan. Bring to boil and, before serving, stir in chopped parsley or chives and season with pepper.

Mamma mia soup

This soup makes a real meal. If you are vegetarian you can omit the bacon and add a chopped tomato for flavour.

SERVES 4–6

1 slice lean bacon
1 stick celery
2 medium zucchini
1 carrot
a little olive oil
a 400 g (14 oz) can cannellini beans
2 cups water
½ cup pasta (e.g. butterfly or wheel-shaped)
1 tbsp chopped parsley
1 tbsp grated parmesan cheese
1 clove garlic, finely chopped (optional)
a little freshly ground black pepper

METHOD

Trim bacon of fat and chop finely.

Wash celery and zucchini, and peel and wash carrot. Cut vegetables into slices.

Brush a saucepan with oil and gently fry bacon, celery and carrot for a few minutes. Add zucchini, stir well, and add beans with their liquid. Add the water, bring to boil, and boil for 2 minutes before adding pasta. Cook until pasta is just done.

A moment or two before serving stir in parsley, parmesan, garlic and pepper.

COOKING TIP

It takes fifteen seconds a day to sharpen a knife with a steel, then cutting is a breeze; practice makes perfect.

PASTA AND MORE

Butterfly pasta with salmon

This pasta dish can be served for lunch or even as an entrée for a special dinner.

SERVES 3–4

1 can salmon in oil, about 200 g (7 oz)
400 g (14 oz) butterfly pasta (preferably
   wholemeal)
about 150 g (5½ oz) mushrooms
1 clove garlic, chopped
1 tsp capers, chopped
1 tomato, diced
freshly ground black pepper
1 tbsp grated parmesan cheese

METHOD

Strain salmon and reserve oil.

Bring a large pot of lightly salted water to the boil and cook pasta in boiling water till *al dente,* i.e. still firm. Slice washed mushrooms.

Heat salmon oil in a saucepan and gently fry garlic and capers for a few seconds. Add mushrooms and stir-fry for a minute before adding tomato to cook for 3 to 4 minutes. Crumble salmon into pan, season with pepper, and stir before tossing with pasta.

Sprinkle with grated parmesan and serve.

COOKING TIP

When preparing a pasta dish for a main course, allow about 100 g dry pasta per person.

Fettuccine with spinach and tomato sauce

Italians love using vegetables as an accompaniment to pasta. Try this one – it's really special.

SERVES 4

1 bunch spinach
4 large tomatoes (or a small can peeled tomatoes)
1½ tbsp olive oil
1 clove garlic, chopped
300–400 g (11–14 oz) fettuccine
a little freshly ground black pepper
1 tbsp roasted pine nuts
1 tbsp grated parmesan cheese

COOKING TIP

Always have canned tomatoes on hand for they can be a short cut to many delicious vegetable dishes, soups and sauces.

METHOD

Detach spinach leaves from stems and wash several times in a large amount of cold water. Drain and shred coarsely.

Place fresh tomatoes in a bowl and cover with boiling water. After 10 seconds place tomatoes in cold water to cool. Remove cores of tomatoes before peeling and halving them, squeezing out the seeds and chopping them.

In a saucepan or wok heat about 1 tbsp of the oil and fry garlic for a few seconds – it must not burn. Add tomatoes and stir-fry for one minute. Then add spinach and stir-fry until it shrinks and darkens.

Meanwhile cook fettuccine in boiling water, referring to packet instructions. Drain and return it to pan. Season with pepper and mix in remaining oil, pine nuts, and the spinach and tomato sauce.

Sprinkle with grated parmesan and serve.

Tagliatelle with vegetables and herbs

The choice of vegetables used here is really a matter of taste and may depend on the season or what you have in your refrigerator. If you do have time to plan, the following suggestions can produce beautiful flavours and colours.

SERVES ABOUT 4

1 cup broccoli, cut into small pieces
1 tomato
½ red capsicum
½ brown onion
1 small eggplant or zucchini
8 mushrooms
1 tbsp olive oil
1 clove garlic, chopped
1 tbsp finely sliced basil
2 tbsp chopped parsley
300–400 g (11–14 oz) tagliatelle
1 tbsp pine nuts
2 tbsp grated parmesan cheese

METHOD

Wash broccoli and steam or microwave it until just cooked but still firm.

Halve tomato and, after squeezing out the seeds by hand, dice the flesh.

Wash capsicum, remove seeds and slice it finely.

Peel onion and slice finely.

Wash eggplant or zucchini and slice finely.

Wash and slice mushrooms.

In a large wok or frying pan heat oil and stir-fry capsicum, onion, eggplant or zucchini and mushroom until soft. Add broccoli, tomato, garlic, basil and parsley. Gently stir well for 30 seconds, then turn off heat and keep warm until pasta is cooked.

Cook tagliatelle according to packet instructions. Gently stir drained pasta, vegetables and pine nuts together and serve sprinkled with a little grated parmesan.

Lentil and silverbeet curry

This aromatic dish is lovely with bread, especially the
Indian type.

SERVES 4–6

a little polyunsaturated oil
½ brown onion, chopped
1 clove garlic, chopped
2 tsp curry powder
½ tsp cummin powder
2 large tomatoes, diced
½ cup orange lentils
½ cup green lentils
1 small carrot, chopped
about 2 large handfuls silverbeet leaves
chilli paste to taste (optional)

METHOD

Brush a large saucepan with oil, add onion and garlic and stir while cooking on medium heat for 2 or 3 minutes without browning. Add curry powder and cummin and stir for about 1 minute. Add tomato and stir well, then add rinsed lentils and chopped carrot.

Cover with water and bring to boil. Put lid on pan and simmer until lentils are almost cooked (20 to 35 minutes), adding a little more water during cooking if necessary.

Meanwhile wash silverbeet two or three times in a large quantity of cold water. Add drained spinach to lentils. Cover pan and cook until spinach has softened – it takes only a few minutes. Stir spinach and lentils and season with chilli paste; serve with bread.

A popular Indonesian noodle dish

There are many versions of this satisfying noodle and vegetable dish, traditionally called 'bami'.

SERVES 4

150 g (5½ oz) Asian noodles or vermicelli
½ onion
1 rasher bacon, trimmed of fat
3 cloves garlic
1 stick celery
1 zucchini
1 large carrot
¼ cabbage
1 egg
a little sunflower or other polyunsaturated
   oil
300 g (11 oz) lean minced beef
1 tsp chilli sauce, or more if you wish
1 tbsp soy sauce
freshly ground black pepper

METHOD

Cook noodles for 3 minutes in boiling water. Strain and refresh under cold tap. Put aside.

Wash vegetables. Dice onion and chop bacon. Chop garlic. Dice celery, zucchini and carrot and shred cabbage.

Beat egg with a little water. Brush a small frying pan with oil and quickly scramble egg in it. Put aside.

Brush wok with a little oil and place on high heat. Fry onion until just brown around the edges. Using an egg lifter, transfer it to a bowl. Next, fry bacon until crisp and add to bowl with onion.

Fry chopped garlic for only 5 seconds before adding minced meat. Fry until loose and browned, then transfer meat to bowl.

If necessary, brush wok with a little oil, and place celery, zucchini, carrot and cabbage in wok. Stir-fry for a few minutes before adding noodles and all cooked ingredients. Season with chilli sauce, soy sauce and pepper, and serve from the centre of the table.

FISH, CHICKEN, MEAT

Fillets Côte d'Azur

This dish can be varied in many ways. The recipe has a Mediterranean flavour and uses herbs, but if you want an Asian touch try using ginger, soy sauce and curry spices. Slice the vegetables finely so that they will cook quickly.

SERVES 4

**about 16 leaves of flat-leaved parsley or 4
  small sprigs curly parsley**
8 slices tomato
freshly ground black pepper
12 basil leaves, shredded
8 mushrooms, sliced
**4 fish fillets of your choice, about 150 g (5 oz)
  each**

METHOD

Wash and slice parsley.

Preheat oven to 200°C/400°F.

Cut four strips of foil each about 25 cm (about 10 in) square. In the centre of each place two slices of tomato, season with a little pepper, and top with a little basil and a few slices of mushroom. Then add parsley and fish fillet and season with more pepper. Lastly, sprinkle with more basil and mushroom. Fold foil to seal fish parcels tightly and place in oven to cook for 8 to 10 minutes, depending on the thickness of the fish.

COOKING TIP

Fish is a good friend to the busy cook: choose whole fish with bright red gills and clear eyes, and ask your fishmonger to clean it for you.

Chinese-style baked fish

Ask your fishmonger to gut and scale the fresh fish you select. Fish belonging to the snapper family is always delicious prepared this way, and you can serve it with rice and watercress.

SERVES ABOUT 4

2 tsp honey
1 tsp peanut or other polyunsaturated oil
1 small hot chilli, seeded and finely sliced
1 tsp grated ginger
1 tsp lemon juice
½ tsp sesame oil
1 tbsp salt-reduced soy sauce
a 1 kg (about 2 lb) whole fish, gutted and scaled
2 spring onions, cut into 2.5 cm (1 in) pieces

METHOD

In a small bowl thoroughly mix honey, peanut oil, chilli, ginger, lemon juice, sesame oil and soy sauce.

Rinse the inside of the fish and pat it dry using a clean towel. Make five or six shallow crosscuts about 1 cm (1/3 in) deep on both sides of the fish. This helps it to cook evenly.

Preheat oven to 200°C/400°F.

Brush fish all over with marinade. Place fish in a greased oven dish and cook in preheated oven for about 20 minutes. Cover fish tail with a small piece of foil during the cooking if it starts browning too much.

Carefully transfer fish with any pan juices to a serving dish and sprinkle with spring onion.

Easy curried fish cutlets

Cutlets rather than fillets are best in this dish because they do not break up too much when cooked. Serve them with brown rice.

SERVES 4

4 medium ripe tomatoes
2 tsp curry powder
1 tsp turmeric
¼ tsp fennel seeds
¼ tsp chilli paste
4 firm fish cutlets, about 150 g (5 oz) each
2 tbsp coriander leaves

METHOD

Preheat oven to 180°C/350°F.

Cut tomatoes into 1 cm (⅓ in) slices and use half of this sliced tomato to line the base of the oven dish.

Mix curry powder with turmeric, fennel seeds and chilli paste then coat fish cutlets with the mixture. Sprinkle half the coriander leaves over sliced tomato in dish and lay spiced fish cutlets on top. Sprinkle remaining coriander leaves over fish and top with remaining tomato slices.

Bake in preheated oven for 15 to 20 minutes or until fish is cooked through.

Scallops with tomato and basil

This is a dish for a special occasion, perhaps an alfresco lunch. It is wise to order fresh scallops from your fishmonger.

SERVES 4

about 600 g (1¼ lb) fresh scallops
a 400 g (14 oz) can peeled tomatoes
2 tsp olive oil
½ medium white onion, chopped
1 clove garlic, chopped
½ cup dry white wine
about 15 basil leaves, finely sliced
1 tsp margarine or butter
freshly ground black pepper

METHOD

Briefly rinse scallops in cold water and remove any rubbery parts or intestine.

Chop tomatoes finely.

In a large non-stick frypan heat half the oil and gently fry onion for about 2 minutes. Stir in garlic and tomatoes, add wine and boil for about 5 minutes.

In a second non-stick pan heat remaining oil and on high heat brown scallops for about 30 seconds on each side. Add scallops and basil to tomato sauce, stir in butter, season with pepper and serve immediately.

COOKING TIP

A few herbs from the garden, snipped over pasta, into soup or onto salads and meat, can add instant flavour.

Italian fish kebabs

Once cooked, fish kebabs should be served immediately, otherwise they lose their moisture and delicate flavour. Ask your fishmonger for a firm fish such as gurnard, flathead or tuna. Allow 2 hours for the fish to marinate before cooking, and remember to soak your bamboo sticks for at least 30 minutes beforehand to prevent them burning. Once on the grill, the fish is ready in minutes.

MAKES ABOUT 8 KEBABS

600 g (1¼ lb) firm fish fillets
1½ tbsp olive oil
1 tsp lemon juice
2 tsp finely chopped onion
2 tbsp finely sliced basil
a pinch of salt
freshly ground black pepper
½ tsp paprika

METHOD

Cut fish into approximately 3 cm (1½ in) cubes and add to a bowl containing olive oil, lemon juice, onion, basil, salt, pepper and paprika. Allow to marinate for about 2 hours.

Thread fish onto bamboo sticks or skewers and cook on a hot barbecue, turning kebabs over halfway through the cooking. They need about 2 minutes on each side and during the cooking they can be brushed with any leftover marinade.

Serve immediately with good bread and rice, and a mixed salad.

COOKING TIP

Salads made from raw vegetables such as zucchini, carrot and beetroot are healthy and quickly prepared.

Poached rainbow trout with a lemon sauce

Rainbow trout has a firm and appetising pink flesh. The fish always comes clean from the fishmonger and you need only scale it before cooking.

SERVES 4

1 glass dry white wine
a few parsley stalks
4 rainbow trout, about 200 g (7 oz) each
1 tbsp olive oil
juice of 2 lemons
2 tbsp chopped parsley
freshly ground black pepper

METHOD

Put wine and parsley stalks in a frypan large enough to hold the four trout. Place fish in pan and cover pan with a lid or foil. Bring to boil, turn heat down low and poach-steam fish for about 12 minutes.

In a small saucepan gently heat oil, lemon juice and parsley. Season with pepper and when the sauce is hot remove it from stove.

Lift trout from pan, peel off skin if you wish, pour lemon sauce over fish and serve immediately.

Mediterranean tuna cutlet

For this main-course dish you need a large casserole that will hold both the fish and the vegetables, and which is suitable for stove-top as well as oven cooking.

SERVES 4

a 600–800 g (1¼–1¾ lb) tuna cutlet
a little flour
1 tbsp olive oil
1 small brown onion, diced
1 clove garlic, chopped
2 sprigs thyme
1 zucchini, diced
1 small eggplant, diced
1 tomato, diced
1 bay leaf
freshly ground black pepper

METHOD

Coat tuna lightly with flour.

Heat olive oil in a casserole dish and on high heat brown tuna on both sides for a couple of minutes.

Preheat oven to 180°C/350°F.

Transfer cutlet to a plate. Add onion, garlic and thyme to casserole dish and fry for about a minute. Add zucchini, eggplant, tomato and bay leaf and cook for a couple of minutes before placing fish cutlet on top. Season with pepper and spoon some of the vegetables onto the fish. Cover dish and bake in oven for about 30 minutes or until tuna is cooked. The fish is ready when the flesh can be easily detached from the bone.

COOKING TIP

A bay leaf taped inside the lid of flour or cereal containers should keep the weevils away.

Pan-fried fish fillets for the family

Ask your fishmonger to fillet a fresh fish for you. Give the kids the tail end, which usually has fewer bones.

SERVES 4

600 g (1¼ lb) fish fillets
a little plain flour
a little freshly ground black pepper
1 tbsp olive or other polyunsaturated oil
2 tsp lemon thyme, chopped (optional)
juice of 1 lemon

COOKING TIP

Scissors are easier than
a knife for trimming
fins from fish.

METHOD

Cut fish fillets into four pieces, lightly coat with flour and season with pepper.

Heat oil in a frying pan just large enough to hold fish. Place fillets in hot oil, skinless side facing down, and cook first side for 2 to 6 minutes, depending on thickness. Sprinkle lemon thyme over fish and refrain from moving it around too much during cooking. If the fish is colouring too quickly, reduce heat. Turn fish and cook second side, adding a little more oil if really necessary.

Finish the cooking and pour lemon juice over fish when it is still in pan. Serve immediately, perhaps with brown rice and finely sliced mixed vegetables.

An exotic Thai fish curry

The distinguishing feature of a Thai fish curry is its use of salty fish sauce and lots of chilli. However, using these ingredients in moderation will still result in a dish with lovely flavours. Brown rice goes well with it.

SERVES 4

400 g (14 oz) firm fish fillets
a little polyunsaturated oil
1 small onion, chopped
2 cloves garlic, chopped
1 tsp ground lemon grass
1 tsp ground cummin
1 tsp ground coriander
1 tsp ground turmeric
1 chilli pepper, halved and seeded, or ¼ tsp
   chilli paste
½ tbsp fish sauce
1 tbsp water
2 tbsp roasted peanuts, finely chopped

METHOD

Remove skin and bones of fish and cut into bite-size pieces or strips.

Heat a little oil in a hot wok and stir-fry onion and garlic until onion looks transparent, taking care not to burn it. Add all spices and mix well before adding fish to stir-fry for a few minutes. Add fish sauce and water and stir well.

Serve hot with finely chopped roasted peanuts sprinkled on top.

COOKING TIP

Learn to use a wok: stir-frying is one of the quickest and easiest of cooking methods.

A multi-purpose curry sauce

*A curry sauce can be adapted to suit your mood or the
ingredients with which it will be served: fennel can be
added for fish, cummin for pulses, coriander for fish and
vegetables, parsley for almost anything.*

SERVES 4

½ brown onion
a 2.5 cm (1 in) piece of ginger
2 cloves garlic
4 tomatoes
2 tsp peanut oil
4 fennel seeds
10 cummin seeds
2 tsp curry powder
½ tsp chilli paste (optional)
1 tbsp desiccated coconut or 1 tbsp finely
   sliced coriander leaves

METHOD

Peel onion, ginger and garlic then blend them
together to a fine purée. Alternatively, chop them
finely.

Halve tomatoes. Squeeze out the seeds and chop
flesh finely.

In a medium saucepan place oil, fennel seeds,
cummin seeds and puréed onion, ginger and garlic.
Cook on low heat for at least 5 minutes while stirring
with a wooden spoon. If ingredients start to burn add
a tablespoon or two of water. Add curry powder and
stir for about 1 minute before adding tomato. Bring to
a simmer and cook on low heat for about 10 minutes,
stirring occasionally.

About a minute before serving stir in chilli paste, and
desiccated coconut or coriander.

One-pot rice and chicken casserole

*This is an excellent example of a meal cooked in one pot –
easy for the cook and even easier for those who wash the
dishes!*

SERVES 4

1 small onion
1 red capsicum
2 tomatoes
a little olive oil
4 skinned chicken thighs
1 cup shelled peas
1½ cups brown rice
3 cups water
freshly ground black pepper
a little saffron, or sweet paprika, turmeric,
    cummin or curry

METHOD

Peel and slice onion, and wash and dice capsicum.

Wash and dice tomatoes.

Brush a wide-based saucepan with a little oil and cook onion, garlic and capsicum for 3 minutes. Add chicken thighs and cook for a few minutes, then add tomato, peas, washed rice and 3 cups water. Season with black pepper and a pinch or two of saffron or a spice of your own choice.

Simmer till rice is cooked (about 35 to 50 mins – read instructions on pack). Add a little water during cooking if necessary.

COOKING TIP

Cook extra rice for
tomorrow's soup, salad
or stuffed vegetables.

Chicken fillets with a golden sauce

Chicken fillets are the most popular of all chicken cuts and, according to my poulterer, it is because 'they are fast to cook and children like them'. No need for any other reason! You can serve the fillets without the sauce for children with unsophisticated palates.

SERVES ABOUT 4

½ red capsicum
1 cup pumpkin flesh, cut into cubes
3 tbsp water
a little peanut or other polyunsaturated oil
4 chicken fillets
juice of ½ lemon
2 tbsp chopped parsley
1 tbsp grated parmesan cheese
freshly ground black pepper

METHOD

Wash capsicum and remove seeds, then dice it.

Place diced capsicum and pumpkin cubes in a saucepan with the water; cover and cook until pumpkin is soft. It takes about 5 minutes.

Meanwhile brush a frying pan with a little oil and, when it is hot, cook chicken fillets for about 5 minutes on either side, using medium heat.

Meanwhile blend capsicum and pumpkin with their cooking liquid to a smooth sauce, adding a little water if necessary.

When the chicken is cooked, add lemon juice to pan and shake lightly before adding the vegetable sauce. Reheat and serve chicken sprinkled with parsley and parmesan and seasoned with a little pepper.

Yummy drumsticks

We have cooked this dish many times at home and our children love it. For best results put the drumsticks on a rack to allow oven heat to circulate around the meat and cook it evenly. If preparing this dish for adults you may wish to add ¼ tsp of chilli and 1 tsp of grated ginger.

SERVES 4

1 tsp honey
1 tbsp salt-reduced soy sauce
juice of ½ lemon
½ clove garlic, finely chopped
¼ tsp sesame oil
freshly ground black pepper
4 chicken drumsticks

great

METHOD

Preheat oven to 180°C/350°F.

In a small bowl mix together honey, soy sauce, lemon juice, garlic, sesame oil and a little pepper.

Skin drumsticks and coat with the marinade preparation. Place drumsticks on a rack, turning them over halfway through the cooking. Cook for about 30 minutes or until chicken is tender, and serve with stir-fried green vegetables and Asian noodles.

Speedy chicken burgers

Burgers can be made from all types of lean minced meat, and the secret of success is a good seasoning. As you will see in this recipe, your lean meat burgers stay moist if you combine the meat well with a little cold water. Minced meat deteriorates rapidly so it is best to cook burgers on the day of purchase. Make your burgers flat, not fat, to speed the cooking time. Serve them with wholemeal rolls and salad.

SERVES 4

¼ brown onion
500 g (about 1 lb) lean minced chicken
1 tbsp dried breadcrumbs
1 tbsp chopped parsley
1 tbsp bottled or home-made Italian tomato
  sauce (see following page)
3 tbsp water
freshly ground black pepper
a little plain flour
a little olive oil

METHOD

Peel onion and chop very finely.

In a bowl thoroughly mix onion, minced chicken, breadcrumbs, parsley, tomato sauce, water and a little pepper. This is best done by hand. Divide the mixture into four and shape into burgers. Coat burgers with a little flour.

Brush a small frying pan with olive oil and cook meat on both sides for 3 to 4 minutes. The chicken meat must be cooked through but not dry.

COOKING TIP

An efficient way to reduce fat consumption when frying is to brush the pan lightly with oil rather than pouring it on.

Italian tomato sauce

I hope every one of you will try this sauce, which I learnt from Silvana, an excellent Italian cook. It can be used with pasta, meatloaf, fish etc., or on pizzas and pancakes. It is best when freshly made but will keep for two or three days in the fridge; busy cooks might like to make double the quantity and freeze some.

SERVES 4

4 to 5 medium tomatoes
½ brown onion
1 stick celery
1 medium carrot
10 leaves basil or a small sprig thyme
1 clove garlic
freshly ground black pepper
1 tsp olive oil (optional)

METHOD

Cut all vegetables into small pieces and place in a saucepan with herbs, garlic and pepper. Cook on medium heat for 20 to 30 minutes.

Remove herbs and pass sauce through a mouli or fine strainer. Check seasoning and stir in olive oil before serving sauce warm.

At the end, if you wish, add more pepper and freshly chopped herbs like basil, tarragon or coriander.

COOKING TIP

If a vegetable sauce is a little too sweet, add some lemon juice, freshly ground black pepper or chilli powder.

Spicy chicken casserole

This is a delicately spiced chicken dish with strong contrasts in colour and texture. It is quite easy to make, and with some fast-cooking Asian noodles or brown rice you will have an exotic and nutritious meal.

SERVES 4

600 g (1¼ lb) small skinless chicken pieces
   on the bone
1 tbsp plain flour
about 300 g (11 oz) French beans
1 red capsicum
1 small brown onion
½–1 tbsp peanut oil
½ tsp turmeric
½ tsp curry powder
1 cup water
1 tbsp desiccated coconut
1 tbsp raw peanuts
freshly ground black pepper
a few fresh coriander leaves

METHOD

Coat chicken pieces with flour.

Wash and halve beans. Halve, seed, wash and finely slice capsicum.

Peel onion and slice finely.

Heat oil in a large saucepan, brown chicken pieces for a few minutes, then transfer them to a plate. Add onion to pan and gently cook for 2 minutes before adding beans, capsicum, turmeric and curry powder. Stir for about 2 minutes to prevent burning. Add water and chicken pieces, then stir again and bring to boil. Reduce to a simmer, cover, and cook for 25 minutes or until chicken is tender.

Add coconut and peanuts, season with a little pepper, stir gently, and cook uncovered for a further 5 minutes. Sprinkle with coriander leaves and serve.

Gingered chicken stir-fry

This dish has exquisite Asian flavours and the satisfying texture of noodles.

SERVES 4

600 (1¼ lb) chicken pieces, preferably with
  bones
2 tbsp grated ginger
1 tbsp soy sauce
juice of 1 lemon
1 tsp sesame oil
125 g (4½ oz) Asian noodles
½ red capsicum
¼ medium cabbage
1 tbsp sunflower or other polyunsaturated oil
½ cup water
freshly ground black pepper

METHOD

Remove skin from chicken and, using a cleaver, cut flesh into bite-size pieces. In a bowl stir chicken with half the ginger, the soy sauce, the lemon juice and the sesame oil.

Add noodles to boiling water and cook for about 5 minutes until they loosen a little. Stir noodles with a fork to separate them, then strain and refresh in cold water.

Wash and chop capsicum. Wash and shred cabbage, discarding large stalks.

Heat oil in wok, add ginger and chicken pieces, and stir-fry on high heat for a few minutes. Transfer chicken to an oven dish and keep it warm in the oven (150°C/300°F). Stir-fry capsicum and cabbage for a few minutes. Add water, cover with a lid or foil, and cook for 3 minutes or until cabbage is just slightly crunchy. Mix in chicken and noodles, reheat, and season with a little pepper before serving.

Paella with chicken and prawns

Paella is a traditional Spanish rice dish garnished with vegetables, chicken and shellfish; it is easy to prepare. An added bonus for busy cooks and their families is the fact that it only requires one saucepan, so even cleaning up is easy.

SERVES ABOUT 4

1 small brown onion
1 clove garlic
1 red capsicum
1 tomato
1 tbsp olive oil
4 small chicken thighs, skinned
1 cup shelled peas
1 cup basmati rice
3 cups cold water
2 pinches of saffron
freshly ground black pepper
8–12 green prawns

METHOD

Peel and finely slice onion.

Peel and crush garlic.

Halve, seed and wash capsicum.

Wash and dice tomato.

Heat oil in a heavy saucepan and brown chicken pieces. Add onion and garlic, stir-fry for 1 minute then add capsicum, tomato, peas, rice and water. Bring to boil and season with saffron and a little pepper. Stir gently, cover, and simmer for 15 minutes.

After this time add prawns, stir gently, cover, and cook for a further 5 minutes. Add a little extra water towards the end of cooking if necessary.

Serve from a large bowl in the centre of the table, perhaps accompanying it with a green salad.

Lamb chops Italian-style

Here is a very quick and simple dish of lamb chops with a
difference, a dish that the tang of the herbs and lemon
transforms into a delightful meal. Serve with cauliflower
and steamed potatoes.

SERVES 4

8 loin lamb chops
a little olive oil
1 small clove garlic, chopped
1 tbsp chopped parsley
1 tbsp finely sliced basil
½ lemon
freshly ground black pepper

METHOD

Trim chops of all visible fat.

Brush a frying pan with a little olive oil and on medium heat cook chops on both sides until almost done. Turn off heat. Drain as much fat as possible from frying pan and, leaving chops in pan, cover with a lid or foil and leave chops to rest for 1 minute.

Return pan to high heat, stir in garlic, parsley and basil and stir well before squeezing a few drops of lemon juice over chops. Season with a little pepper and serve.

COOKING TIP

Once meat is in the pan, avoid moving it constantly because this slows the cooking process.

Stir-fried beans with minced beef

This dish shows that vegetables can be the principal ingredient of a satisfying main course. Asian noodles or mashed potato would make a delicious accompaniment.

SERVES 4

600 g (1¼ lb) thin French beans
1½ tbsp polyunsaturated oil
1 small brown onion, finely chopped
1 clove garlic, chopped
about 300 g (11 oz) minced beef
1 tbsp dark soy sauce
2 tbsp water
¼ tsp sesame oil
a little chilli paste (optional)

METHOD

Wash beans and top and tail them by hand, removing any strings at the same time. Slice beans diagonally into several pieces.

Heat 1 tsp oil in hot wok and stir-fry onion and garlic until onion is transparent. Add meat and stir-fry until it has changed colour. Stir in soy sauce and transfer to a plate.

Add remaining oil to wok and stir-fry beans for 1 minute. Add water by pouring it down the side of the wok; cover wok and cook for about 2 minutes. After checking that beans are cooked, stir in sesame oil, and a little chilli paste if you wish. Stir in cooked beef and reheat before serving.

COOKING TIP

If food is pleasantly seasoned during cooking there will be little inclination to add salt at the table.

Curried lamb with vegetables

This is a mild curry, so if you prefer it with more flavour, increase the quantity of curry powder or add a little hot chilli to the dish at the beginning. There is little work involved in the dish but you need to plan ahead because it takes about 2 hours to cook.

SERVES 4

2 tsp polyunsaturated oil
¼ tsp cummin seeds
2 cardamom pods
½ brown onion, chopped
2 cloves garlic, chopped
1 tbsp grated ginger
2 tsp curry powder
½ tsp turmeric
400 g (14 oz) lean lamb, cubed
1½ cups chopped tomato
2 medium zucchini
2 medium carrots

METHOD

Heat oil with cummin seeds and cardamom pods in a heavy saucepan and gently fry onion, garlic and ginger for a couple of minutes. Add curry powder and turmeric and stir well before adding trimmed cubes of lamb. Stir again well until meat starts to brown and is well coated with spices. Add tomato and stir well. Cover pan and simmer for about 1 hour.

Cut zucchini and peeled carrots into bite-size pieces and add to curry. Cook for a further 45 to 60 minutes or until lamb is tender. Serve with brown rice.

Curry powder

Grind to a powder 4 tbsp coriander, 1¼ tbsp cummin, 1 tbsp fenugreek, 1½ tbsp turmeric, 1 tbsp black peppercorns, 6 dried chillies and 10 cardamom seeds. Blend the spices together well (you get about ¾ cup) and store in an airtight jar away from sunlight.

Asian beef with snake beans

Snake beans are the very long ones favoured by many Asians. Our children love this stir-fry, and my wife Angie and I find it very fast.

SERVES ABOUT 4

300 g (11 oz) rump steak
1 tbsp salt-reduced soy sauce
1 tbsp dry sherry
1 tsp cornflour
400 g (14 oz) snake beans (or French beans)
200 g (7 oz) Asian noodles
1 tbsp peanut or other polyunsaturated oil
½ clove garlic, crushed
1 thin slice ginger
¼ cup water
1 tsp hot chilli paste

METHOD

Trim beef of all fat and cut into bite-size strips. In a bowl mix beef with soy sauce, sherry and cornflour.

Bring a large saucepan of water and a medium saucepan of water to the boil. Wash, top and tail beans, cutting them into 5 cm (2 in) pieces. Place beans in boiling water of large saucepan for 1 minute. Drain beans.

In the medium saucepan cook noodles in boiling water, following packet instructions.

Heat two-thirds of the oil in a wok. Add garlic, slice of ginger and the beef and stir-fry until meat has browned. Transfer meat to a plate and discard ginger.

Pour remaining oil into wok and stir-fry beans for about 15 seconds before pouring ¼ cup water down the wok.

Stir well, cover, and cook until beans are tender but still crunchy. Then add beef, noodles and chilli paste, or serve chilli paste separately if you wish; stir well to reheat and serve.

Lamb casserole with a difference

Here is a no-fuss dish, one to share with your best friends. The cinnamon and cloves give it a touch of the unusual, and the peas and macaroni make a whole meal of it. This winter casserole takes a little over an hour to cook but very little time to prepare.

SERVES 4

600 g (1¼ lb) lean lamb meat (preferably from leg or shoulder), trimmed and cut into cubes

a little olive oil

1 brown onion, diced

2 cloves garlic, crushed

1 can (about 400 g/14 oz) tomatoes

2 cloves

1 bay leaf

a 2 cm (¾ in) stick of cinnamon

freshly ground black pepper

2 cups macaroni (preferably wholemeal)

500 g (about 1 lb) peas

METHOD

Brush the bottom of a good saucepan with a little olive oil. Add diced onion and fry for a few minutes, stirring with a wooden spoon. Add garlic and cubed meat and cook for a few minutes more. Add tomatoes, cloves, bay leaf and cinnamon. Season with pepper, cover, and cook until meat is almost tender (approximately 1 hour). Add macaroni and shelled peas, then cover with boiling water taken from the kettle. Stir and cook until macaroni is ready.

Discard cinnamon, bay leaf and cloves if you can find them.

COOKING TIP

The tougher cuts of meat become succulent when marinated: cut the meat into small pieces and put them into the marinade the night before stir-frying or barbecuing.

Stir-fried beef with broccoli

Here is a model dish on which to practise your stir-frying technique. Broccoli is a classic vegetable to serve with beef.

SERVES 4

300–400 g (11–14 oz) rump steak
2 tsp dark soy sauce
2 tsp dry sherry
2 tsp cornflour
400 g (14 oz) broccoli
1 tbsp polyunsaturated oil
½ clove garlic, chopped
1 small carrot, sliced
1 small brown onion, cut into pieces
¼ cup water
200 g (7 oz) Asian noodles
2 tbsp roasted, skinned almonds
3–4 drops sesame oil

METHOD

Trim beef of all fat and cut into bite-size strips. In a bowl mix beef with soy sauce, sherry and cornflour. Put aside.

Wash broccoli. Cut it into florets and then into bite-size pieces.

Heat two-thirds of oil in a wok and stir-fry meat and garlic until meat is browned. Transfer to a plate.

Pour remaining oil into wok and stir-fry carrot and onion for 1 minute. Then add broccoli and stir before adding water, taking care to pour it down the side of the wok. Stir well, cover and cook for a few minutes until cooked but still crunchy.

Meanwhile cook noodles according to packet instructions – they require only a few minutes.

Add meat to vegetables and stir well, adding almonds and sesame oil. Serve over cooked noodles.

Tandoori loin of lamb

To prepare the meat, ask your butcher to debone 4 racks of lamb each with three or four chops, or do it yourself. All fat and skin must be removed so that your loin is very lean. As an alternative, ask your butcher for some lamb or mutton backstrap – about 150 g (5 oz) of meat per person. The meat needs to marinate for at least 1 hour but the result is really tender, spicy lamb. I sometimes make the marinade the night before and it only takes me 15 minutes to finish the dish.

SERVES ABOUT 4

2 tsp low-fat natural yoghurt
1 tsp grated ginger
¼ tsp freshly ground black pepper
½ tsp paprika
½ tsp cummin seeds
1 tsp curry powder
¼ tsp chilli powder
1 tsp peanut or other polyunsaturated oil
½ tsp lemon juice
4 pieces deboned loin of lamb about 10 cm (4 in) long

METHOD

In a small bowl thoroughly mix yoghurt, ginger, pepper, paprika, cummin seeds, curry powder, chilli powder, oil and lemon juice. Rub all sides of loin of lamb with this spicy preparation and leave to marinate in a cool place for 1 to 4 hours.

Preheat oven to 250°C/500°F.

Cook loin in hot, preheated oven on an oven rack resting in an oven dish for about 15 minutes. Turn loin over two-thirds of the way through the cooking. To help save time later with the washing up, place a sheet of foil under your oven rack.

Serve with rice or Asian noodles and steamed green vegetables.

COOKING TIP

Buy your spices in small quantities: they lose their aroma and freshness once they have been ground.

Grand-mère Gourdon's pork chops

Just thinking of this dish reminds me of my childhood. Pork is the meat most often eaten in France, and at home we ate pork chops much more frequently than lamb chops. Avoid overcooking pork, which tends to become dry when overdone.

SERVES 2

1 Granny Smith apple
2 tbsp water
2 pork chops
a little peanut or other polyunsaturated oil
½ brown onion, sliced
freshly ground black pepper

METHOD

Peel, quarter and core apple. Place in a small saucepan with the water, cover, and cook until apple is soft.

Trim pork chops of all visible fat. Brush a frying pan with a little oil and on medium heat fry chops on both sides until almost cooked. Remove chops from pan, place on a dish and keep warm in the oven (at 100°C/210°F).

Add sliced onion to pan and cook until soft. Then add cooked apple to pan, stir well, season with a little pepper and reheat briefly.

Remove chops from oven. If there is any liquid in the dish, add it to the apple sauce then spoon sauce over chops and serve with green vegetables.

Creative meatloaf

*Create your own meatloaf, using your favourite
ingredients and experimenting with various seasonings.
Remember to mix it very well to obtain a good texture.*

SERVES 4

1 small brown onion
1 clove garlic
2 tbsp chopped parsley or
  ½ tsp chopped thyme
400 g (14 oz) lean minced beef, chicken or
  pork
½ cup chopped carrots
½ cup chopped celery
1 egg
½ cup breadcrumbs
½ cup water
2 pinches of cummin powder (optional)
2 pinches of grated nutmeg
freshly ground black pepper

METHOD

Chop onion, garlic and parsley or thyme.

Preheat oven to 220°C/450°F.

Put all ingredients in a large mixing bowl. Season well with pepper and, using both hands, mix well for a minute or so.

Place mixture in a greased oven dish, brush top with water and bake in preheated oven. After 10 minutes reduce heat to 180°C/350°F and cook for a further 20 minutes.

Remove from oven and allow to rest for 10 minutes before serving from the centre of the table accompanied by a seasonal green vegetable and pasta, potatoes or rice.

Spicy lamb kebabs

I suggest cooking the kebabs in a hot oven, but you can of course do them on a barbecue. If using bamboo or wooden sticks, soak them in water for 30 minutes before putting in the oven, to prevent them burning.

SERVES 4

2 tsp low-fat yoghurt
¼ tsp paprika
¼ tsp chilli paste
½ tsp cummin
½ tsp curry powder
¼ tsp freshly ground black pepper
1 tsp sunflower oil
500 g (about 1 lb) cubed leg of lamb (bite-size pieces)
1 capsicum
1 medium onion
16 small mushrooms

METHOD

In a small bowl mix together yoghurt, paprika, chilli paste, cummin, curry powder, black pepper and oil. Stir lamb cubes into marinade and keep in a cool place for 4 to 6 hours.

A short time before cooking, preheat oven to the hottest temperature possible.

Halve, seed and wash capsicum and cut into squares about the same size as the lamb pieces. Cut onion similarly. Quickly wash mushrooms.

Thread meat cubes and vegetables onto sticks. Cook in oven on an oven rack until just done, remembering to turn kebabs over halfway through the cooking.

Serve on a bed of rice from a central dish.

Happy endings

Judging by the enormous popularity of dessert recipes, most of us seem to be very partial to sweets. In this section you will find quick-to-prepare desserts that are mostly based on fruit and low in both fat and added sugar. I have included fruit salads, crumbles, iced fruits, loaves, cakes and muffins. There is a recipe for everyone and for every season!

WAYS WITH FRESH FRUIT

Berry and plum salad

Once you know the principle of this fruit salad you can be creative with other fruits.

SERVES 4

½ cup raspberries
½ cup blueberries
½ cup blackberries
juice of 1 orange
juice of ½ lemon
1 tsp honey
1 small bunch fresh sultana grapes
3 blood plums

METHOD

Mash or blend half the raspberries, blueberries and blackberries, then stir in fruit juices and honey.

Add washed grapes then the blood plums, each cut into eight pieces. Add remaining berries.

Stir gently and serve, or refrigerate until required.

COOKING TIP

Eat lots of fruit, vegetables and wholegrain cereals to keep kilojoule and fat consumption moderate.

Exotic fruit salad

This is a fruit salad for all occasions, but at home we especially enjoy it after spicy food. We also use it to show off the culinary delights of Australia to overseas visitors.

SERVES 6

2 slices pineapple, 1 cm (1/3 in) thick
juice of 2 oranges
2 passionfruit
1 tbsp sugar
2 bananas
¼ small pawpaw
1 small custard apple
6 rambutans or lychees

METHOD

Trim and core pineapple slices and blend to a liquid with orange juice. Place in a bowl and add passionfruit pulp, sugar, sliced bananas, and peeled and sliced pawpaw.

Open custard apple and gently scoop out the white flesh, avoiding the mushy pulp just under the skin. Discard seeds and add custard apple to bowl.

Peel rambutans or lychees, remove seeds and add to bowl.

Refrigerate fruit salad. Remove from refrigerator at least 20 minutes before serving to allow the fruit to return to room temperature.

COOKING TIP

Choose tropical fruits by smelling them, and store them in your fruit bowl rather than in the refrigerator.

Mango and berry delight

Everyone will find this fruit salad exotic. Those who live in the tropics will consider raspberries and blueberries a treat, and those living in a temperate climate will adore the mango. The beauty of the dish is its natural flavour, and I'm sure you will agree that no sugar or cream is necessary.

SERVES 4

1 large mango
3 passionfruit
2 nectarines
½ cup raspberries
½ cup blueberries
juice of 1 orange

METHOD

Peel mango and slice thinly into a salad bowl.

Halve passionfruit and add to bowl.

Cut washed nectarines into thin segments and add to fruit salad. Gently stir in raspberries, washed blueberries and orange juice. Cover and refrigerate if you are not serving it immediately.

COOKING TIP

When berries are plentiful, freeze them by spreading on trays in the freezer, then storing them there in tightly sealed freezer bags.

Blackberries with a pear and apple sauce

This dessert is very popular at our place in autumn, at the beginning of the new apple and pear season when blackberries are still around. You can, of course, replace the blackberries with other fruit such as strawberries. It is special enough to serve to friends – stylish, yet simplicity itself to make.

SERVES 4

1 pear
1 apple
a few drops lemon juice
2 tbsp water
1 tsp sugar
2 tbsp low-fat natural yoghurt
1 tbsp low-fat milk
250 g (9 oz) blackberries
1 tsp bitter cocoa powder (optional)

METHOD

Peel, quarter and core pear and apple. Halve apple pieces and place, along with pear, in a saucepan with lemon juice and water. Cook on medium heat until soft. Blend to a very fine purée with sugar. Allow to cool.

Whip yoghurt with milk for a few minutes to lighten it, then mix this into pear and apple purée.

Place blackberries in serving bowl and spoon pear and apple sauce on top. Shake the bowl.

Refrigerate until required, and dust with cocoa if you wish before serving.

COOKING TIP

Provide fresh fruit and raw vegetables for children to help them cut down on between-meal snacks of biscuits, cakes and lollies.

Granny Smith apple tart

A French apple tart is often made with puff pastry, but for this one I use the much lighter filo pastry and the result is lovely.

SERVES ABOUT 6

5 Granny Smith apples
2 tbsp water
3 sheets of wholemeal filo pastry
a little peanut oil
1 tbsp low-fat cream
1 tbsp castor sugar
2 tbsp apricot jam or a little icing sugar from
   a shaker (optional)

COOKING TIP

Keep filo pastry in its
packet until you need
it; any left over can be
tightly sealed and
stored in the
refrigerator.

METHOD

Peel, quarter and core one apple and cook with 2 tbsp water in a covered pan until apple is soft. Mash and allow to cool. (If you spread purée on a plate it will cool more quickly.)

Peel, halve and core remaining four apples. Cut thinly into 2 mm (1/10 in) slices.

Line a baking sheet with 1 sheet of filo pastry. Brush it with a little oil and place another sheet of pastry on top. Again brush with oil and place a third sheet of pastry on top. Preheat oven to 220°C/450°F.

Stir cream into cold apple purée and spread this over pastry. Beginning at one corner, place apple slices on top of purée. The apple slices should overlap so as to leave no gaps and you'll probably have some apple left over. Sprinkle apple slices with castor sugar and cook in a hot oven for 15 minutes. The pastry should be crisp and the edges of the apple slightly browned.

Before serving, brush with warm apricot jam or dust with icing sugar.

Rhubarb and raspberry crumble

A fruit crumble is a treat and full of goodness. The main fruit here is rhubarb, but you can also use apricots or pears with other berries. Rhubarb is available throughout the year but is at its peak in summer. The crumble is cooked in a gratin or oven dish big enough to serve six people.

SERVES 6

3 cups diced, peeled rhubarb
1 tbsp grated orange rind
1 apple
1 tbsp water
1 tbsp castor sugar
6 tbsp rolled oats
1 tbsp plain wholemeal flour
1 tbsp desiccated coconut
1 tbsp chopped raw almonds
1 tbsp polyunsaturated margarine or butter
1 tbsp honey
250 g (9 oz) raspberries (or other berries)

METHOD

Place rhubarb and rind in a saucepan with peeled, quartered and diced apple and the water. Cook on medium heat until apple and rhubarb are just soft. Stir in castor sugar.

Thoroughly combine rolled oats, flour, coconut, almonds, margarine and honey. This is best done by hand.

Preheat oven to 210°C/430°F.

Spoon apple and rhubarb into oven dish and top with raspberries. Spread crumble mixture over fruit and pat down a little. Place dish in oven and cook for 10 to 15 minutes or until the top is golden brown.

Serve hot or cold.

Baked spring fruits

Apricots and cherries are two very seasonal fruits. I look forward to them each year and enjoy preparing this delicious dessert.

SERVES 4

1 tsp butter or margarine
8 ripe apricots
20 cherries
½ cup water
1 tbsp brown sugar
4 tbsp slivered almonds

METHOD

Preheat oven to 200°C/400°F, and butter a gratin or oven dish.

Wash and halve apricots; wash cherries and remove stones. Place apricot halves in oven dish. Dot with cherries, pour water over fruits and sprinkle with sugar. Bake for 20 minutes or until apricots are very soft.

Lightly brown almonds in a warm frying pan and sprinkle over baked fruit just before serving.

COOKING TIP

Avoid stoning fruits such as cherries and apricots too early as they oxidise and develop an unpleasant taste and colour.

Pear and orange sorbet

Pears are best in the autumn months when their sweet perfume is most charming.

SERVES 8

5 William pears
1½ cups water
juice of 1 lemon
4 tbsp sugar
grated rind of ½ orange
grated rind of ½ lemon
3 drops vanilla essence

METHOD

Peel, quarter and core pears. Place in a saucepan with water, half the lemon juice, sugar, orange rind and lemon rind. Bring to a gentle boil, cover, and simmer for about 10 minutes or until pears are just soft. Allow to cool. Add remaining lemon juice and vanilla essence, and blend pears and liquid to a very fine purée.

Place purée in icecream maker and make your sorbet. Store in the freezer in a covered bowl or in an icecream container with a lid.

If you don't have an icecream maker, place preparation in a stainless-steel bowl in freezer. When purée starts to set, whisk it for 10 to 15 seconds and return to freezer. Repeat this procedure until the purée is too hard to whisk. The whisking lightens the sorbet.

LOAVES AND CAKES

Walnut and date loaf

This is a nice moist loaf that keeps well for several days.

MAKES 12 SLICES

1½ cups wholemeal self-raising flour
½ cup sugar or honey
a pinch of salt
1 tsp cinnamon
1 cup chopped walnuts
1 cup chopped dates
1 cup grated apple
1 cup water
60 g (2 oz) butter or polyunsaturated
 margarine

METHOD

In a bowl combine flour, sugar or honey, salt, cinnamon, walnuts, dates and apple.

Preheat oven to 180°C/350°F.

Bring water and butter to boil and, using a wooden spoon, mix this with other ingredients. Spoon into greased loaf tin approximately 20 cm (8 in) long and bake in preheated oven for 45 minutes.

COOKING TIP

It is energy-efficient to make two loaves instead of one; freeze the second loaf, tightly wrapping it in a freezer bag.

Banana and pear loaf

Slices of this fruity loaf, low in fat, make a popular snack for children and fit neatly in a lunchbox.

MAKES 12 SLICES

¾ cup water
½ cup diced dried pears
60 g (2 oz) butter or polyunsaturated
  margarine
½ cup honey
1½ cups wholemeal self-raising flour
a pinch of salt
½ tsp ground cinnamon
½ cup chopped almonds
½ cup sultanas
1¼ cups grated banana

METHOD

Bring water, pears and butter to boil. Remove from heat and stir in honey.

Mix together flour, salt, cinnamon, almonds and sultanas in a bowl.

Preheat oven to 180°C/350°F.

Using a wooden spoon, mix the first preparation into the second, adding the banana at the same time. Spoon into a greased loaf tin approximately 20 cm (8 in) long and bake in preheated oven for 40 to 50 minutes.

COOKING TIP

Look for fruits canned in natural juices, an excellent pantry standby for healthy desserts in a hurry.

Tropical fruit cake

This exotic, moist fruit cake is best cooked in a greased rectangular loaf tin. It contains no added sugar or fat but is rich, and a small slice is satisfying.

MAKES ABOUT 12 SLICES

200 g (7 oz) diced dried pawpaw
200 g (7 oz) dried mango
20 dried apricots
5 dried pear halves
2 cups water
2 medium bananas
2 cups wholemeal self-raising flour
½ cup chopped raw almonds
¼ tsp cinnamon

METHOD

Place dried pawpaw, mango, apricots and pears in a saucepan with the water. Bring to boil and simmer for about 5 minutes. Strain off liquid and blend it with 10 of the apricots, and the bananas, to a fine purée.

Preheat oven to 180°C/350°F.

Transfer fruit purée to a mixing bowl and incorporate flour, almonds and cinnamon. Spoon a quarter of this cake mixture into greased loaf tin 20 cm (8 in) long. Top with half of pawpaw and mango, then add another quarter of cake mixture. Top with remaining whole apricots and pears, then add another quarter of cake mixture. Top with remaining pawpaw and mango and finish with remaining cake mixture.

Tap tin to ensure that it is properly filled, and flatten top of mixture using a wet spoon.

Bake in oven for about 50 minutes. Allow to cool a little before unmoulding onto a cake rack.

Serve with a berry sauce made by blending fruit such as blueberries and raspberries with orange and lemon juice plus castor sugar. It needs to be strained to remove the seeds.

Apple and sultana muffins

The secret of a good muffin is speed – the faster you prepare them the better they taste. Our children particularly like apple and sultana muffins.

MAKES ABOUT 12 MUFFINS

a little melted margarine
1 large apple, Granny Smith or Golden Delicious
3 tbsp sultanas
a pinch of cinnamon
2 tbsp honey
1½ tbsp polyunsaturated oil
¾ cup low-fat milk
1 cup wholemeal self-raising flour
½ cup white self-raising flour

METHOD

Brush muffin tray with melted margarine.

Preheat oven to 200°C/400°F.

Peel, core and dice apple, and place it in a bowl with sultanas, cinnamon, honey, oil and milk. Gently mix to dilute honey.

Place the two kinds of flour in a large bowl. Pour the apple and liquid preparation onto the flour and, using a wooden spoon, stir until just combined: it is important not to overmix. Spoon this preparation immediately into your muffin tins and bake in preheated oven for 15 to 20 minutes. When muffins are cooked, turn them out onto a wire rack.

INDEX